Send all inquiries to:
In Celebration
3195 Wilson Drive NW
Grand Rapids, MI 49544

ISBN 0-7647-1042-7

1 2 3 4 5 6 7 8 9 10 STP 09 08 07 06 05 04

MOSES
AND
THE VERY SPECIAL BASKET

Written by Sunny Griffin
Illustrated by Linda Welty

Long ago there was a wicked king who didn't like any of the Israelites, especially the baby boys.

Moses' mother knew God would help save her baby boy from this wicked king.

Miriam, Moses' big sister, loved her little baby brother very much.

Moses' mother made a very special basket that would float on the water.

She hid Moses in the very special basket on the river where Miriam could watch it.

When the king's daughter and her maidservants came to the river to bathe, they found the very special basket.

A maidservant took the very special basket out of the water and handed it to the princess.

The princess took baby Moses out of the very special basket and hugged him.

Miriam rushed over to the princess and told her about a nurse for the baby.

The nurse Miriam brought to the princess was Moses' very own mother.

The princess loved baby Moses and raised him in the palace as her own son.

Moses' mother thanked God every day for letting the king's daughter be the one to find her very special basket.

Moses grew up and trusted God, just like his mother had done when he was a baby!